T0208136

Dream Conversations

ALSO BY THOMAS CLEARY

The Blue Cliff Record (1977, 1992)*

The Flower Ornament Scripture (1984-1987, 1993)*

Shōbōgenzō: Zen Essays by Dōgen (1986)

The Buddhist I Ching, by Chih-hsu Ou-i (1987)*

Zen Essence: The Science of Freedom (1989)*

Zen Lessons: The Art of Leadership (1989)*

Transmission of Light, by Zen Master Keizan (1990)

The Book of Serenity: One Hundred Zen Dialogues (1991)

*The Japanese Art of War: Understanding the
Culture of Strategy* (1991)*

No Barrier, by Wumen (1993)

Rational Zen: The Mind of Dōgen Zenji (1993)*

Zen Antics: One Hundred Stories of Enlightenment (1993)*

Zen Letters: Teachings of Yuanwu (1994)*

*Published by Shambhala Publications

Dream Conversations

On Buddhism and Zen

Musō Kokushi

Translated and edited by

Thomas Cleary

SHAMBHALA

BOULDER

1996

SHAMBHALA PUBLICATIONS, INC.
2129 13th Street
Boulder, Colorado 80302

Shambhala Publications makes every effort to print on acid-free, recycled
paper.
Shambhala Publications is distributed worldwide by Penguin Random
House, Inc., and its subsidiaries.

The Library of Congress catalogues the previous edition
of this book as follows:

Musō Soseki, 1275–1351.
[Muchū mondōshu. English]
Dream conversations on Buddhism and Zen/Musō Kokushi: translated
and edited by Thomas Cleary.
p.   cm.   (Shambhala Centaur editions)

ISBN 978-1-57062-206-9

1. Zen Buddhism—Doctrines—Early works to
1800.   I. Cleary, Thomas F., 1949–   .   II. Title.
III. Series.
BQ9268.M8513   1994   93-39949
294.3'927—dc20   CIP

BVG 01

CONTENTS

TRANSLATOR'S INTRODUCTION

Eight hundred years ago the history of the Japanese nation and people was altered forever. Impatient with an effete, self-absorbed aristocracy, the upper-class military elite established its own central paragovernment, thus inaugurating a series of martial regimes that were to keep Japan in thrall for centuries to come.

Seating their government in Kamakura, hundreds of miles from the ancient imperial capital in Kyoto, the chief warlords of the new order also distanced themselves from the culture of the old aristocracy. Patronizing Zen Buddhism and neo-Confucianism, newly imported from China, the Kamakura government sought to revolutionize the culture of Japan in such a way as to undermine both the material and spiritual foundations of the old order.

This influx of Chinese culture from the splendid Southern Sung dynasty was boosted in the late thirteenth century by the fall of that dynasty to the Mongolian conqueror Kublai Khan. Chinese refugees from the mainland to Japan during those times included people of culture and learning, even some Zen masters, who were cordially welcomed by the leaders of the military government.

Not all of the reverberations of contemporary events in China were welcome in Japan. Once the whole of continental China had been taken by the Mongol warriors, Kublai launched further invasions, to the south and the east. Invasion forces reached southern Japan by sea in the late 1270s and early 1280s, to be repelled once, it is said, by a *kamikaze* ("spiritual wind"), a natural storm defending the rocky coast from aggression, and once by a valiant collaborative defense staged by heroic warriors from all over Japan.

Ironically, the salvation of Japan from the Mongolian invasion also planted seeds of the downfall of the military regime. Under feudal custom, successful valor in battle was rewarded by land grant. So many were the illustrious deeds of the Japanese heroes in the defense of the nation from Kublai's fleets, however, that there was no way to compensate them all adequately in the traditional manner under the conditions of the time.

The resulting drain on natural resources and the inevitable disgruntlement of some warrior clans helped to undermine the stability of the regime. Civil wars eventually broke out, and the imperial house even attempted to recover some authority from the military rulers. When the dust cleared temporarily in the 1330s, a new group of warriors had attained sufficient dominance to establish a new military government. In contrast to the earlier regime, these new shoguns made their capital in Kyoto, the old imperial city, and attempted to further develop the Zen-based new high culture in closer harmony with classical Japanese Buddhist culture.

The first of the Kyoto shoguns was Ashikaga Takauji. While military and political rivalry persisted between the new shogun and his younger brother, Ashikaga Tadayoshi, the two demonstrated greater harmony in the domain of cultural reconstruction and development. Both warriors became disciples of Musō Soseki, one of the greatest Japanese Zen masters of the age. Under Musō's Zen influence, commercial and cultural relations with China were expanded, the classical doctrines of ancient Japanese Buddhism were reconciled with Chinese Zen and other religious developments, and new schools of literature and art flourished, thus boosting the evolution of Japanese civilization during a critical time in its political history.

This Zen master Musō was teacher not only of the shogun but also of the emperor, from whom he thus received the honorific title of Kokushi, or National Teacher. So great was the repute of Musō Kokushi, in fact, that he was thus entitled by several successive imperial courts; including posthumous honors, Musō was awarded the title Kokushi by no fewer than seven emperors.

Raised from childhood in the esoteric Shingon (Mantric) school of Japanese Buddhism, Musō later studied Zen with both Chinese and Japanese Zen masters. His first Zen teacher, I-shan I-ning, had been an ambassador from Yuan dynasty China; he was also the Zen teacher of Sesson, one of the greatest painters in Japanese history. Musō's main Japanese teacher, Kohō, had been an imperial prince who left the worldly life to learn Zen from Wu-hsueh Tsu-yuan, another transplanted Chinese master. Musō himself became a highly skilled teacher, producing more than fifty enlightened disciples, a most unusual number.

Musō's teaching was largely based on the great *Tsung Ching Lu* (Source Mirror Record), a massive Chinese collection of extracts from the Buddhist canon combining the teachings of the various schools with the message of Zen. Although this comprehensive text still exists, it is unfortunately no longer studied in Japanese Zen schools, which subsequently became alienated from orthodox canonical Buddhism and involuted into cultic sects.

Most of what is known of National Teacher Musō's teaching is today found in *Muchū Mondō,* or *Dream Conversations,* which is a collection of Musō's written replies to questions of Ashikaga Tadayoshi about Buddhism and Zen. Written in an easy, nontechnical style, *Dream Conversations* explodes misconceptions about Zen with unprecedented clarity, replacing standard myths with fundamental psychological insights and exercises designed to lead the lay individual into the depths of Zen experience.

This volume presents the first English translation of National Teacher Musō's letters. Although the language and style of the original text are very easy for those well versed in Japanese culture, nevertheless some of the material deals with matters of strictly local concern, and the diction is often somewhat prolix in order to buffer the impact of the Zen barb on a military leader in a feudal regime. Some discussions, therefore, bear on issues that are no longer relevant, or are couched in terminology proper to a world view that no longer exists in Japan and has never existed in the West.

Most of the psychological and spiritual problems outlined and resolved in this text are, nevertheless, common to people of all cultures and times who attempt to conquer the self and master the mind. The confusion into which modern Buddhism has fallen, particularly in the West, makes the incisive teachings of Zen master Musō not only relevant but critical to the rediscovery and effective application of Buddhist spiritual technology. In order to preserve and pass on the effective content of the text without the excess baggage of outdated material, therefore, the concern of this translation has been not merely to render the work into English but also to extract and present the quintessential message in such a way that it is not obscured by the medieval trappings of its historical origins.

Dream Conversations

LIBERATION

Those who seek liberation for themselves alone cannot become fully enlightened. Though it may be said that one who is not already liberated cannot liberate others, the very process of forgetting oneself to help others is itself liberating.

Therefore those who seek to benefit themselves alone actually harm themselves by doing so, while those who help others also help themselves by doing so.

COMPASSION

There are three kinds of compassion. One kind is compassion whose object is living beings as such. Another is compassion whose object is elements. The third is objectless compassion. These three kinds of compassion are very different.

The compassion whose object is living beings as such is the compassion of one who thinks beings are real and their delusions are real, and who wishes to liberate these real beings from their real delusions. This is sentimental compassion, which is limited by feelings. It is still just emotion and desire, not real liberative compassion.

The compassion whose object is elements is the compassion of one who sees all beings as conditional productions of causal relations, as compounds of elements that have no real person or thing in themselves. This is illusory compassion for illusory beings, using illusory means to liberate illusory beings from illusory delusions. Although it transcends the sticky emotion of sentimental compassion, this dreamlike compassion still retains the image of illusion, so it is not yet truly liberated compassion.

AIM IN LIFE

There is ultimately no means of safeguarding anything in this world; anything you gain can be lost, destroyed, or taken away. For this reason, if you make the acquisition and retention of goods or status your aim in life, this is a way to anxiety and sorrow.

PAST, PRESENT, AND FUTURE

It is a characteristic tendency of human beings to indulge in emotions such as happiness, grief, or anger in response to present conditions, failing to balance these feelings with the awareness that present conditions are results of past causes. It is illogical to face the present only as an object of enjoyment or tolerance, neglecting to use it as the opportunity to create the future.

CAUSES

Causes are complex and have different time scales. The efforts of the individual are not the sole determining factor in the individual's condition in life, because everyone is part of the nexus of society and nature and the continuum of time. It is common for people to attribute causes wrongly because of misperception of real relationships.

Every cause is the effect of something else, and every effect is the cause of something else. What may seem a curse may be a blessing, and what may seem a blessing may be a curse. Hardship is a blessing when it spurs effort and development; ease is a curse when it increases complacency and self-indulgence.

ENLIGHTENMENT AND FEELINGS

If you forget your feelings about things of the world, they become enlightening teachings. If you get emotional about enlightening teaching, it becomes a worldly thing.

CONTAMINATION OF VIRTUE

Doing good seeking rewards is contaminated virtue. Doing good without thought of reward, dedicating it to enlightenment, is uncontaminated virtue. Contamination and noncontamination refer to the state of mind of the doer, not to the good deed itself.

THE INEXHAUSTIBLE TREASURY
OF POTENTIAL

There is a vast potential, latent within human beings, that remains undiscovered because of the limitations placed on consciousness by habitual preoccupations. The recommendation that all cravings be relinquished does not mean that detachment itself is a goal; it is a means of breaking through self-imposed restrictions and opening up this inexhaustible treasury of potential.

GREED

Just as greed for worldy things is inhibiting and self-defeating, so also craving for otherworldly things prevents the opening of the mind.

HELP IN DISGUISE

When people are unsympathetic to you and the world does not go as you wish, this should be a help to detachment of feelings from the repetitious cycle of becoming and decay, gaining and losing.

ANSWER TO PRAYER

The withholding of divine aid from those who would become presumptuous, more attached, more indulgent, and more shameless if their wishes were fulfilled is itself divine aid to such people. In a corrupt age, when prayers are not answered, that is itself the answer.

PITY

The pity of great saints for ordinary people is not necessarily because of the wretchedness of the human condition in itself but more because of the great potential humanity has and does not use, the high estate from which humanity has fallen.

THE CENTRAL BENEFIT OF ZEN

The central benefit of Zen, in the context of the ordinary ups and downs of life, is not in preventing the minus and promoting the plus but in directing people to the fundamental reality that is not under the sway of ups and downs.

VIRTUE WITHOUT WISDOM

Virtue without wisdom is said to be an enemy for three lifetimes. When the time is passed in ignorance, doing only contaminated good, virtue in hopes of reward, it is therefore not possible to clarify the true ground of mind. This is the enemy of the first lifetime.

As a result of contaminated virtue, pleasurable states eventually develop. Still in the realm of emotion, they occasion a deepening of mundane attachments. These attachments become influences toward greedy and possessive behavior. This is the enemy of the second lifetime.

When the pleasurable states are worn out, while the force of ignorance has not been diminished but rather increased by habitual attachment to the rewards of virtue, the fall from the state of elevation of feeling produces negative reactions. This is the enemy of the third lifetime.

RELIGIOUS AND SECULAR INSTITUTIONS

Religious institutions might be supported for secular ends, while secular institutions might be supported for spiritual ends. It is important to discern this distinction in reference to both types of institution.

THE GROUND OF MIND

As long as people have not realized the basis of mind, even if they do good works their virtue is contaminated. This is why teachers of Zen and other schools of Buddhism have recommended that people first clarify the basic ground of mind and then cultivate virtues after that.

The good cultivated by people who have not realized the essence of mind is only the cause of fabricated results. Therefore it is not the essential way to liberation. Even if they teach and initiate others, they fall into sentimental compassion, so it is not true guidance.

DEMONS

There are various mental phenomena and mental postures that obstruct the potential for true understanding. Because of their harmful and destructive nature, they are called demons or devils.

These demons include greed, hatred, conceit, opinionated views, addiction to meditation states, pride in knowledge, desire for personal liberation for one's own sake alone, sentimental compassion, anxious haste to attain enlightenment, idolizing teachers, rejecting the teaching because of finding fault with teachers' external behavior, indulging in passions, and fearing passion.

Anyone who wants to realize Buddhist enlightenment

is obliged to examine his or her mind and heart for these devils.

These demons may arise because of incorrect application of mind. They may also flare up in a correctly applied mind in which they are about to die out, just as a candle flame will flare up just before it goes out. In any case, do not allow the mind to be stirred by demons, because this agitation perpetuates their influence.

SPIRITUAL MALPRACTICE

One may enter into the sphere of influence of demons as a result of spiritual exercises and experiences. This may be likened to the case of a warrior who is rewarded for achievement in battle, then develops an exaggerated sense of self-importance as a result of that reward, eventually to be punished for presumptuous behavior.

When a person takes pride in spiritual practices or experiences, that individual is certain to fall into the sphere of influence of demons. This is not the fault of the practice itself but of the attitude of the practitioner. Those who undertake spiritual practices with wrong ideas, or develop wrong views in the course of practice, and those who become conceited and oppose the doctrines or methods of others, enter states of mind and modes of being that may be referred to as "hell."

RELIGIOUS PRACTICE
OBSTRUCTING ENLIGHTENMENT

A scripture called *Obstacles of Pure Action* explains how religious practices can in fact obstruct the path of enlightenment: this occurs when those who practice almsgiving despise the selfish, when those who observe moral precepts are critical of those who do not, when those who practice forbearance belittle the impatient, when those who practice vigorous diligence look down on the indolent, when those who practice meditation reject the distracted, and when those with knowledge make light of the ignorant.

It is not that the practices are themselves the work of demons but that acquisitiveness in the practitioner converts religious practice into self-approval and condemnation of others, which obstructs the course of enlightenment.

POSSESSION

People who undertake spiritual exercises with a sense of acquisitiveness, even with regard to "spiritual states," are really doing the work of demons, even if they feel they are being spiritual. Those who seek knowledge and extraordinary powers for the sake of personal gain and fame are also doing the work of demons.

When people are possessed by such inner demons, they

may become receptors of external forces that artificially boost their intellectual or psychic powers for a time. Not realizing that it is a false and deceptive condition, such people attribute this to themselves and become all the more conceited and possessed by their demons.

MEDITATION AND MADNESS

People sometimes go mad from doing Zen meditation. This may happen when some perception or understanding arises through meditation, and the practitioner becomes conceited about it. It may also happen when the practitioner has unsolved psychological problems. Then again, it can happen through excessive physical and mental strain due to greedy haste to attain enlightenment.

QUELLING DEMONS

A simple method of quelling demons is to refrain from clinging to anything mentally. This is illustrated by an ancient story, in which a strange person used to roam around the grounds of a hermitage of a certain meditation master. Sometimes he would appear as a Buddhist saint, sometimes as a celestial king, sometimes radiating extraordinary light, sometimes uttering strange sayings. This continued for ten years, and then it stopped.

The meditation master told his disciples, "A celestial

demon had been coming here to bother me, but no matter what appearance it created, I dealt with it by not looking or listening. The demon's manifestations had an end, but my not looking and not listening have no end."

PASSING THROUGH THE DEATH EXPERIENCE

A principle similar to that of quelling demons may be applied to the problem of passing through the experiences of dying.

An ancient Zen text recommends that when people are dying they should contemplate their mental and physical elements as being void of ultimate reality, having no independent being and no identity of their own.

Further, they should contemplate the true mind as being formless, neither coming nor going, the essence of mind not coming into existence at birth and not going out of existence at death, being forever tranquil.

By this means, people can leave the world; they will not be drawn to beatific visions or frightened by horrific visions, such as they may experience at death according to their mental states. The mind will be forgotten and merged with the cosmos.

AVERSION AND ATTACHMENT

Aversion or fear of demonic states is itself a demonic state. If you have emotional attachment to the appearances of the state of Buddhahood, then it is actually a demonic state. If you are unconcerned by the appearances of demonic states, then they are the realm of Buddhahood.

True practitioners of Buddhism are not emotionally attached to the realm of Buddhahood and do not fear the realms of demons. If you work in this way, without conceptualizing realization yet without becoming bored, obstructions will vanish of themselves.

INHERENT KNOWLEDGE

A primary aim of Zen is the uncovering of what is known as inherent knowledge. This is not the kind of knowledge that is produced by thinking based on conditioned consciousness. It is said that the ignorant are obstructed by ignorance, while intellectuals are obstructed by intellectual knowledge.

One way of getting past these obstacles and approaching inherent knowledge is to let go of whatever comes to mind.

SUPERSESSION

Even the many grades of spiritual knowledge progressively realized on the Way are to be superseded. All these stages of spiritual progress are like medical treatments for ailments, which are no longer to be used after they have taken effect and health is restored.

Thus it is said that knowing previous errors along the way is what makes the subsequent superseding states.

SCHOLASTIC LEARNING

Scholastic learning can be a definite hindrance to real knowledge, especially when it is associated with self-importance. This applies both to literalists and to theoretical interpreters.

In Buddhist terms, to be learned in the real sense means to understand meaning. The real meanings of Buddhism are beyond conceptual images and verbal expressions.

TYPES OF KNOWLEDGE

There are various kinds of knowledge as defined in Buddhism. There is genuine knowledge and false knowledge, temporal knowledge and true knowledge. People often think of religious knowledge as understanding of doctrines; conventional knowledge or ignorance, however, are not knowledge and ignorance in the true sense.

It has been said that the Path is not in knowledge or nonknowledge. Enlightenment is not merely a matter of intellectual understanding, nor yet of obliterating intellectual understanding and being empty and calm.

A way to approach the fundamental knowledge is to set aside all such interpretations and focus intensive nonconceptual inquiry on the state where this setting aside has taken place.

PRACTICES AND STAGES

The definition of practices and stages is for the benefit of people of middling and lesser faculties. The development of knowledge is an important practice insofar as it is an instrument for those who cannot as yet merge directly with inherent fundamental knowledge.

Instrumental knowledge is likened to a raft that carries you to the shore of the fundamental. Those who cling to the raft and will not let go of it are those who do not know the real importance of the raft.

People of the highest potential are as if able to fly and thus are not in need of a raft to get to the other shore beyond delusion. They can reach the fundamental directly, without using the knowledge of the various stages. To encourage such people to acquire scholastic learning of religion is like giving a raft to someone who can fly; it will only be a hindrance.

WRONG APPROACH

Because it is said in Zen teaching that academic intellectual knowledge is not attainment of truth, there are those who think they will accord with the true Way by abandoning learning and intellectual understanding. This is also a wrong idea, which blocks the Way.

The Flower Ornament Scripture says, "All beings have the knowledge and virtues of Buddhas, but they cannot realize this because of wrong ideas and attachments." Suppose there is a man who is strong and talented but because of a serious illness becomes weak and forgets his abilities. Seeing a healthy person exercising skills, no longer realizing he himself originally had this ability and strength too, the man becomes envious and attempts to train himself to perform. This just tires him out and aggravates his illness.

If this man would first cure his illness, believing that he originally had these skills and strength, now suppressed by illness, then his powers would become manifest as before.

So it is with Buddhist study. Although the knowledge and virtues of Buddhas are inherent in everyone, people are unable to experience and use them because they are obstructed by the illness of wrong ideas and delusions. If they do not realize this fact and become envious at seeing or hearing of sages exercising the powers of knowledge and virtue, and so they study all kinds of books, memorize sayings, seek spiritual powers, and wish for intellectual excellence, this will all increase their sickness of wrong ideas, and their inherent knowledge and virtue will not become manifest.

STANDARD MISCONCEPTIONS

There are a number of common misconceptions about Buddhism and what it teaches. Summarized as follows, they may generally be found wherever word of Buddhism has been heard:

1. The pure land and the defiled land, or paradise and the mundane world, are separate; delusion and enlightenment, ordinary people and sages are not the same.

2. There is no difference between sages and ordinary people, no distinction between the pure and the defiled.

3. In Buddhist teaching there are distinctions such as greater and lesser, temporary and true, exoteric and esoteric, meditation and doctrinal study.

4. Buddhist teachings are completely equal, none better than another in any way.

5. All activity and perception is itself Buddhism.

6. Buddhism exists apart from all activities.

7. All things really exist.

8. All things are impermanent.

9. All things are either eternal or pass away entirely.

10. All things are illusory and empty, or they are in between existence and nonexistence.

11. There is no truth outside doctrine.

12. There is a truth outside doctrine that is better than doctrine.

All of these represent statements that are to be found in Buddhist views. All of them are partial views that are used for temporary purposes. When they are held as fixed views or sacred dogma, therefore, they turn into misconceptions. In order to understand the Zen frame of mind, it is necessary to suspend fixation on such views or vacillation between them.

MEANS AND END

People who arrive at the fundamental may subsequently teach any kind of doctrine to people as an expedient, without their own understanding being limited to any such doctrine. The intellectual interpretations of these doctrines made by people who have not arrived at the fundamental, however, are all misconceptions.

Thus people may have received all the verbal teachings of the founders of spiritual schools without actually being like the founders. So the transmission of the verbal teachings is obviously not in itself the point of the schools. As an ancient commentary on a scripture says, "Mind itself realizes mind, mind itself awakens mind."

To therefore reject or abandon instruction, however, and just carry on according to how you happen to think and feel is also a wrong idea. Scripture calls this the disease of letting be.

UNDERSTANDING THE ZEN KOAN

The exercise of keeping a Zen saying or story in mind is incompatible with a conscious desire for understanding on your own terms. According to an ancient saying, "Do not consciously seek enlightenment."

This is because the consciousness under such conditions is preoccupied by the desire. The unenlightened mind, furthermore, which by definition does not know what enlightenment is, cannot know what or how to seek.

The koan is not absolutely essential in Zen; it is also just an expedient means, used to transcend the bounds of the conditioned mind. In order to achieve this breakthrough, it is important to bypass the demands of the conditioned mind and approach the koan directly.

THE FUNDAMENTAL

The fundamental is not characterized by intelligence or stupidity in the ordinary sense. Those who are obsessed with such appearances are the stupid, while those who are not are the intelligent.

So those who attain knowledge of the fundamental do not pride themselves in being wise.

MEDICINE AND DISEASE

People do not need medicine when they are well. Medicine is important when they are ill. Physicians diagnose illnesses and prescribe accordingly. Because there are many different illnesses, so there are many different medicines. Nevertheless, despite the variety of medicines, their healing purpose is one and the same, to restore original health.

So it is with Buddhism. In the fundamental state, people have no maladies. They become psychologically afflicted, however, because of ignorance. Their afflictions are various, so the teachings of Buddhism, the remedies for afflictions, are also various. In spite of the variety of Buddhist teachings, all of them have the same purpose, which is to restore people to the well-being of the fundamental state.

Enlightenment does not, therefore, refer to academic knowledge of the various teachings of Buddhism. Enlightenment means having gotten rid of ignorance and attained unconditioned liberation. Teachings may conduce to this, but they are not the experience itself. To approach the teachings as a field of study is what is called turning medicine into disease.

EXPERT ADVICE

When you are ill, if you think you have to study medical science before getting treatment for your illness, you will get sicker and die before you ever finish learning medicine. If you go to an expert physician, however, the physician can diagnose your ailment and prescribe accordingly. As a patient, you may not understand the knowledge underlying the doctor's prescription, but if you follow expert advice, you will get well.

Buddhist practice is also like this. If you try to learn all the doctrines first and then apply them, you might spend a whole lifetime studying the doctrines without learning them all, so many and diverse are they. If you never get around to application, learning is ultimately useless.

Real teachers therefore give students only as much instruction as they need to apply. Even if the students cannot understand immediately, if they keep the directions of the teacher in mind without trying to fit them into preconceived interpretations, when the appropriate time arrives the obscurity should dissolve.

TWO KINDS OF KNOWLEDGE

Enlightened people are sometimes said to have two kinds of knowledge, one called fundamental knowledge and another called acquired knowledge.

Fundamental knowledge is the inner realization of the enlightened. Acquired knowledge refers to the means developed by the enlightened to teach others.

The teachings of the Buddhist doctrines and Zen koans are all expedient means for transforming others; they are not the fundamental knowledge of inner experience. Intellectual understanding gained by students of the doctrines of Zen by reading scriptures or attending the lectures of teachers is all in the realm of acquired knowledge.

If you have actually experienced the inner realization of the enlightened, you may then develop acquired knowledge in order to help others, and expound teachings or meditations to liberate people.

THE PRIORITY OF FUNDAMENTAL KNOWLEDGE

Those who have not realized the fundamental knowledge of the enlightened should first aim to reach the realm of this basic inner realization. In order to accomplish this, it is necessary to transcend the boundaries of doctrine and meditation. Those who keep doctrines or Zen teachings on their minds cannot reach the fundamental.

This is why it is said that realization is only attained when you read the teachings of Buddhas and Zen masters as if they were enemies. It is also said that we should not worry about the branches and just get to the root.

THE BASIS AND THE OUTGROWTHS

When we plant a tree, as long as the roots take, the branches and leaves will naturally grow and the flowers and fruits will develop. Therefore when we plant the tree, we are concerned about the roots and not about the branches and leaves. As long as the roots have not taken a firm hold, we prune off the small branches so that the energy will go to the roots.

That does not mean, however, that we plant the tree for the sake of the roots alone. We take great care with the roots for the sake of the branches, leaves, flowers, and fruits.

SELF-REALIZATION AND TEACHING OTHERS

Even those who have realized the fundamental are still not completely enlightened in Buddhism as long as they do not know the techniques of a living adept. Such people may indeed have correct self-realization, but they cannot function as guides if they lack methodological skills for helping others. This condition is sometimes referred to as attaining the intent but not the expression.

Then again, even though people may have figured out some of the methods of adepts, they themselves cannot be teachers if their own perceptions are not clear. These are people who have reached the expression but not the intent.

INTENT AND EXPRESSION

According to an ancient saying, those who have not yet attained enlightenment should study the intent rather than the expression, while those who have attained enlightenment should study the expression rather than the intent.

The intent is the inner meaning of Zen, which is the fundamental that is inherent in everyone. The expression is the varied methodology of the Zen schools. The intent is the root, the expression is the branches. Students first need to find out the inner meaning of Zen, not getting bogged down in expressions.

MATURATION

After realizing the intent of Zen, people in ancient times used to spend decades polishing themselves thoroughly in order to free themselves from compulsions of conditioning and habit. This is called the work of maturation; the completion of maturation is called the attainment of unification.

LIVING ZEN

After the stage of unification, various subtle capacities and functions appear spontaneously. The methods employed by such adepts for helping others thus derive from freedom; they are not products of conventional learning.

This quality of freedom and spontaneity is referred to as being alive. Such people are said to have attained both intent and expression, and what they say is called the living word.

STABILIZATION OF THE BASIS

When a tree does not flower and fruit in a reasonable time after it has been planted, we know that the roots have not set firmly, so attention must be given to the proper care of the roots above all. If you do not realize the problem is in the roots and just try to make branches grow and flowers bloom, the roots will go on withering all the while you are devoting your attention to the outgrowths.

Similarly, even if you have realized the meaning of Zen, if your capacities and functions have not developed, you still should not devote your attention to these outgrowths. Rather you should dwell on correct mindfulness of the fundamental so as to get rid of the views of personal and religious ego, getting beyond both ordinary feelings and religious experiences, thus thoroughly embracing the fundamental transcending them all.

ATTAINMENT AND PRESERVATION

Since ancient times it has been said that ascertainment of truth is relatively easy compared with the difficulty of preserving truth. Preservation of truth is the work of maturation.

There are aesthetes who have psychic experiences that they take to be real, even though they are not true. Without doing any basic developmental work, such people believe they are fundamentally correct and just need to learn spiritual functions. So they study the teachings of Zen and other Buddhist schools for this purpose. Such study, however, just obscures the fundamental even more. People like this may eventually become obsessed and deranged.

There are also people who have psychic experiences that they believe to be fundamental and take developmental work to mean preservation of altered states. So-called development on this basis just increases ignorance.

ZEN EXPRESSION

The terms *intent* and *expression* originally came from poetics. It might be said, for example, that the phrasing of a poem is very nice but its mentality is insipid.

Zen uses the terms with a different meaning. Zen has various teachings, referred to by such terms as transcendence and integration, the beyond and the here and now, holding still and letting go, arresting and releasing, killing and enlivening, three mysteries, three essentials, five ranks, ruler and minister, and so on. All of these are in the realm of expression.

Some uninformed people refer to understanding the definitions of such teachings as attainment of the intent. They think that mastery of expression means the ability to answer questions easily when explaining these terms to others. What such uninformed people consider to be the intent is in fact still in the realm of expression. To study in this way may appear to be study of both intent and expression, but it is not really so at all.

STUDYING EXPRESSION

Contemplating Zen sayings and stories is not necessarily a matter of studying the expression. Theoretical discussion and assessment of the different modes of teaching, outlook, practice, and experience as represented in the sayings and stories is called studying the expression.

Even if people sit silently facing a wall, if they keep various bits of knowledge and understanding in their minds and try to arrange and assess them, this is also in the realm of study of expression.

STUDYING INTENT

The method of studying intent is to lay aside all intellectual understanding and emotional assessment and look at a saying or story directly.

Even if you are reading records of ancient sayings or listening to a teacher lecture, if you forget what is on your mind and open up, not producing rationalizations of what you are reading or hearing, this is studying the intent.

OUTREACH OF METHOD

Once people have clearly realized the intent of Zen, then the teacher may discuss with them the methods and manners of the various Zen techniques. If people cannot master technique, they cannot work as teachers.

For Zen teachers, knowledge of verbal expression should not be limited to the methods of Zen schools only but should extend to the devices of other Buddhist teachings and even to other philosophies and secular sciences.

ZEN TECHNIQUES

There are many Zen expressions that stand for what may be called positive and negative teachings. These are often used to describe the psychological functions of Zen literature.

Pairs of terms such as holding still/letting go, killing/enlivening, suppressing/fostering, praising/censuring, and so on, are used to indicate alternation, combination, and balance of complementary modes of being such as stillness and activity, transcendence and involvement, weeding and seeding.

Such terms may also be used to refer to specific ways of handling Zen literature in order to bring out usage and meaning appropriate to the needs of a particular individual or community.

HYPOCRITICAL SCHOLARS

Many Buddhist scholars do not actually aspire to enlightenment but really study to enhance their own reputation and prestige and to feed their personal pride. When they get some knowledge, they set themselves up as teachers and fool the ignorant. They tell people their bit of knowledge and interpretation and give formal approval to any scholars whose views correspond with their own. This is a big mistake.

PRACTICAL APPLICATION

According to Buddhist scripture, even if people are learned, as long as they do not put their learning into practice, they are no different from the ignorant. This is also true of mundane activities; to understand the principles and talk about them may be quite easy, but actual performance is not so easy.

Many learned people only profess and do not actually refine their minds. This is why they do not reach the attainments of the sages whose books they study.

When Confucius was alive he taught his students the principles of humaneness, justice, courtesy, intelligence, and truthfulness and had them practice these principles. When Confucius testified that so-and-so had learned humaneness, or so-and-so had learned justice, he was referring to people whose hearts were humane or just, not to people who had merely learned to talk about humaneness and justice but had no humaneness or justice in their hearts.

Later students of Confucianism, however, claimed to be masters of Confucian teaching as soon as they had learned definitions of humaneness and justice, without having cultivated humaneness and justice in their hearts.

The same was also true of Buddhism. When Buddha was in the world, not all of his followers were geniuses who attained liberation promptly and became free, but even those of mediocre and lesser faculties who heeded Buddha's instructions and put them into practice attained benefits according to their abilities. Even after Buddha's death, all those who practiced the teaching appropriately gained some benefit. This was because they followed Buddhism only for liberation and for the salvation of all living beings, not for social status and material profit.

In later times, many people, both laity and clergy, followed and studied Buddhism for the sake of reputation and material profit. Therefore they did not advance in actual self-cultivation and refinement. They thought it was enough to learn the doctrines of the various schools. As a result, the more learned they were, the more conceited they became.

In consequence of all this, whereas ordinary people have just the usual personal ego, students of Buddhism added to that a religious ego. Therefore even scholars of outstanding erudition might be no different from the most wretched miscreants in terms of their actual way of living and manner of being.

Zen teaching says that it is better to practice a little than to talk a lot. Zen masters have therefore recommended that learned understanding be subordinated to study through personal experience.

The time nevertheless came when even Zen students were given to literary pursuits and became so proud of their erudition that they were not ashamed of having no real experience of enlightenment.

ASPIRATION FOR ENLIGHTENMENT

In the Buddhist teachings various distinctions are drawn among aspirations for enlightenment. Essentially, it may be said that there are two kinds of aspiration for enlightenment: the shallow aspiration and the true aspiration.

Understanding that whatever is born must die, that whatever flourishes must decline, forgetting worldly ambitions and only seeking the way to emancipation—this is called the shallow aspiration for enlightenment. The great Buddhist master Nagarjuna said, "To observe the impermanence of the world is temporarily called the aspiration for enlightenment."

Because it is a practice for entering from the shallows to the depths, those in whom even this shallow aspiration for enlightenment does not arise cannot develop the true aspiration for enlightenment. This is why Zen teachers have always explained the principle of transience to their students, even though they point directly to the fundamental.

Those who are merely alarmed by impermanence and give up worldly ambitions but do not develop true aspiration for enlightenment are still ignorant people.

People commonly assume that it is aspiration for enlightenment to abandon worldly ambitions and go to live in a hermitage in the mountains to clear the mind with the sound of waterfalls and the wind in the pines. But this cannot be called true aspiration for enlightenment. A scripture says, "Those who live in seclusion in mountains and forests and think that they are thus better than others cannot even attain happiness, let alone Buddhahood."

True aspiration for enlightenment is development of the mind that has faith in supreme enlightenment. Inherent in everyone, supreme enlightenment is eternal and unchanging. To believe in this is called true aspiration for enlightenment. A scripture says, "From the moment of their first inspiration, enlightening beings only seek enlightenment, with unwavering steadfastness."

Even if you believe in inherent enlightenment, if you only believe and have no inner communion with it, this is not yet actually the true aspiration for enlightenment.

The belief or faith that characterizes the true aspiration is not reposed in a dogma or in an external object; in essence, it is the orientation referred to in the scripture as only seeking enlightenment. This means passing through worldly states without clinging; it also means passing through spiritual states without taking them to be final or absolute.

This progress can only be maintained with an inner sense of the transcendence of enlightenment over lesser goals, coupled with an inner sense of the immanence of this enlightenment in the mind. This fertile union of inner sense is called true aspiration for enlightenment.

Aspiration that is only in the realm of belief, without this inner communion, is what scripture refers to when it says, "This aspiration for enlightenment arises and passes away, is transient; it is not the permanent, indestructible essence of enlightenment."

The aspiration for enlightenment that is an inherent property of every human mind is referred to in scripture by the saying, "In supreme enlightenment there is no past regression, no present regression, no future regression."

The Great Sun Scripture says, "What is enlightenment? It is to know your own mind as it really is." A commentary says, "If the mind itself is enlightenment, why do people not become enlightened? Because they do not know the mind as it really is. If they knew the mind as it really is, they would become truly awakened at the moment of their initial inspiration."

If people who are not yet in communion with the inherent mind of enlightenment consider relentless devotion to religious practice to be evidence of firmness of will for enlightenment and power in practice, they will certainly become obsessed because of their pride. Then again, there is also the anxiety that if this determination weakens and they are distracted by worldly conditions, then they will not attain salvation. Thus inherent enlightenment becomes increasingly obstructed and obscured by this pride and this fear.

When beginning practitioners get into such a frame of mind, if they realize that these erroneous ideas have arisen because they are not yet in harmony with the transcendental path, and if they lay it all aside to look directly into their minds, they will eventually reach accord.

A scripture says, "If people seek enlightenment, they have no enlightenment. To envision enlightenment in some form is to become alienated from enlightenment."

WORLDLY FEELINGS

Attraction and aversion are two feelings that keep people within the bondage of ignorant repetitive behavior. Those who seek only what pleases them and try to avoid what displeases them are acting in this way because they do not realize the nature of the world.

For those who know the nature of the world, lack of complete satisfaction or fulfillment in things of the world is in itself advice to cultivate detachment. If people do not crave to be pleased, they will not be displeased. What causes mental suffering is not the environment itself but the mind itself.

SOFTENING WORLDLY FEELINGS

The founder of Zen spoke of two ways of access to awakening; by principle and by practice.

Access by principle refers to direct unification with the fundamental, without depending on training. Since this is not possible for everyone, the founder also taught four practices.

The first two practices are designed to counteract the tendency to be distracted by feelings related to pleasing and displeasing situations. In displeasing situations, you counteract irritation, resentment, and lament by viewing such situations as products of your own disagreeable behavior in the past. In pleasing situations, you counteract complacency and attachment by reflecting on the impermanence of all conditions.

These two practices are used to equilibrate the mind in order to open the way for unadulterated concentration on higher objectives.

As a scripture says, however, "To stir thoughts is error; to stop thoughts is also error." Stopping thought is not enlightenment, and projecting subjective designs on an unlimited objective cannot lead to success. Therefore the founder taught a third practice, which is not seeking anything. As he said, to be enthralled with anything is to be in thrall to that thing.

Not seeking anything is still not considered ultimate.

Not seeking what you think is there is a doorway to finding out what actually is there, beyond your imagination. Only finding, without seeking, is called meeting the source everywhere.

Keeping in touch with the source in this way is the essence of the fourth practice taught by the Zen founder. This practice, known as accord with reality, is still in the realm of achievement and is not what Zen literature refers to as the great rest.

NO SET TRACK

Zen teaching has no set track or fixed pattern. Sometimes it explains mundane principles, sometimes it expounds transmundane doctrines. In any case, the purpose is to dissolve people's sticking points and relieve them of their bondage. Therefore there is no dogma or doctrinal orthodoxy; the only issue is what will effectively liberate and enlighten people.

According to an ancient Zen saying, "If you understand, you can use it on the road; if you do not understand, it becomes a mundane convention." Even if people are given mystic teachings for transcendence, if they do not understand them, the teachings become conventional doctrines.

On the other hand, if hearing explanation of worldly principles frees people from clinging and bondage, with the result that they unite directly with the fundamental, then these worldly principles are in that sense profound teachings.

WORK ON THE FUNDAMENTAL

It is not necessary to get rid of worldly feelings in order to work on the fundamental. Those who are keenly aware of the precariousness of our situation as human beings and the brevity of our opportunity to awaken, and who use this awareness to hone their will, are not distracted from the work by worldly feelings.

Feelings that arise because of circumstances can actually be used to fuel the urgency of work toward the fundamental. Preliminary methods of softening worldly feelings are taught for the sake of those with insufficient determination. This does not mean that work on the fundamental is to be undertaken only after worldly feelings are ended.

NOT FORGETTING

Even while you call to mind ways of softening worldly feelings when they arise, still you should not give up work on the fundamental. It is said that people with intense determination for enlightenment neglect even to eat and sleep; such people do become tired and do become hungry, but they rest and eat in the midst of the work and therefore are not hindered even when sleeping or eating.

If people who lack such determination go without eating or sleeping, they will become ill. This will hinder their practice, so they are encouraged to eat enough to overcome hunger and sleep enough to overcome fatigue. This does not mean, however, that they should forget the work while eating or sleeping.

An ancient Zen master gives this advice: "When you walk, watch the walking; when you sit, watch the sitting; when you recline, watch the reclining; when you see and hear, watch the seeing and hearing; when you notice and cognize, watch the noticing and cognizing; when joyful, watch the joy; when angry, watch the anger." Working in this way will lead to awakening.

DREAMS AND ILLUSIONS

There is a popular practice, commonly found in Buddhist scriptures and Zen writings, that consists of looking upon all phenomena as if they were dreams or illusions. This practice is in the realm of method and is not an ultimate teaching.

Secular literature and folk sayings use the image of things being like dreams or phantasms to mean that everything is transient. In Buddhism, the implication is that phenomena are ultimately insubstantial but nevertheless conditionally manifest. This represents a balance, avoiding both reification and nihilism. Although things exist, what we perceive of them is not their real existence; although things are void of absoluteness, that knowledge is not really void.

Thus, contemplation of phenomena as dreamlike is an elementary expedient used to facilitate realization of the Middle Way transcending dualistic and extreme views.

The use of this practice in Zen is not for the purpose of getting people to contemplate the principle but to encourage them to set everything aside to turn directly to the fundamental. An ancient master said, "Why bother to try to grasp dreams, phantasms, hallucinations? Abandon gain and loss, right and wrong, all at once."

SETTING ASIDE IS ALSO A MEANS

If you set everything aside and do not keep either Buddhism or the world on your mind, is this what is called the fundamental? The founder of Zen said, "Not pursuing objects outwardly, the mind not panting inwardly, if the mind is like a wall, one can enter the Way."

Another Zen master explained that this means the practice of setting all objects aside and not stirring the mind is an expedient method for entering the Way. Therefore, to take this state itself to be the Way is actually contrary to the intent of the founder of Zen.

NOT JUDGING OTHERS

It is said that people who are truly on the Way do not discuss judgments of others. This does not mean that they make judgments but suppress them; it means they do not see people in terms of self and other. The third patriarch of Zen said, "In the realm of being as is, there is no other and no self." A scripture says, "The nature of reality is like an ocean; you should not say there is right or wrong."

If people view the world in terms of distinctions between others and self, they will inevitably make judgments of right and wrong. If they entertain views of right and wrong, they are not true practitioners of the Way, even if they refrain from expressing their views.

Rather than try to refrain from discussing judgments of others, therefore, students of Buddhism should turn around and reflect, "Who is it that speaks of others' right and wrong?"

A scripture says that people "take the physical constitution to be their own body and take the reflections of sense data to be their own mind." What this scriptural saying means is that what ordinary people think to be their self is not the true self. And if you do not know what your true self is, you cannot see others as they really are either.

So if your ideas of self and of others are both untrue, how can you judge right and wrong?

Ordinarily, people who assume they are on the Way

and do not talk about others' right or wrong still define good and bad in their minds and make distinctions of sharpness and dullness in people. Conceptualizing shallowness and depth of understanding, they contrast error and correctness of practice. Such people cannot proceed directly toward supreme enlightenment, so they are encouraged not to pay attention to judgments of right and wrong.

THE ORIGINAL SELF

Even those who have set aside all judgments of right and wrong and do not view people in terms of self and other cannot be said to be truly on the Way as long as they have not seen the original state before personal history.

A way to see this original state is to turn the attention inward: What is it that distinguishes and defines self and others, body and mind? What is it that thinks of right and wrong and gain and loss?

In ancient times, Nanyue went to the sixth patriarch of Zen. Seeing him approach, the patriarch asked, "What is it that has come in this way?"

Unable to answer, Nanyue withdrew. After eight years of inner reflection, he finally had a great realization.

Returning to the patriarch, Nanyue replied, "It would not be accurate to refer to it as something."

Only then did Nanyue receive the approval of the Zen patriarch.

It may seem that Nanyue's inability to understand and answer immediately shows that he was dull. In actuality, however, the fact that he pursued the question "What is it that has come?" to the very end, and ultimately came back with the answer, is evidence of his sharpness. Without this penetrating inquiry, you can never become enlightened.

When he had finished a lecture and the audience was leaving, a certain Zen master of ancient times used to call to them, and when they turned their heads he would say, "What is it?" He was not teaching them how to meditate, nor was he asking for their views. If people can understand his intent directly, any lack of clarity will disappear at once.

Once there was a Buddhist professor who was widely read in the scriptures and treatises and understood their meanings and principles. He had a following of students and had been professing for a long time when he visited the great Zen master Mazu and asked him a number of questions. The professor did not approve of the Zen master's answers, and so he left. At that very moment, the Zen master called to him; when the professor, then on his way out, turned his head, the Zen master said, "What is it?" With that, the professor suddenly experienced a great awakening.

This professor had studied Buddhist texts for years and had understood their principles conceptually, but he did not have any real experience of enlightenment. Then at one word from the Zen master—"What is it?"—he was greatly awakened. What does this mean? Obviously, what he realized was not merely a doctrine or a principle.

If scholars and intellectuals would take the time they spend on trying to foster learned understanding and apply it to direct inquiry into the place where thoughts arise and vanish, and if they would carry on this inquiry throughout all their activities, they would be able to attain entry into enlightenment just as Nanyue and the professor did.

WRONG APPROACHES

Sometimes people ask about Buddhism and are given the reply, "Who is it that is asking about Buddhism?"

Some people identify themselves based on their customary ideas and say that this self is that "who."

There are also those who think the reply means they should wonder who they are.

Then there are those who latch on to the saying "Your own mind is Buddha" and then pose and gesture as their answer.

Some people fix on the insubstantiality of the cognizing mind, the realm of detachment from all forms, and equate it with Nanyue's statement, "It would not be accurate to refer to it as something." Then their answer is that there is nothing above to reach up to and no self below.

Then again, there are some who have the notion that all questions and answers are extraneous, and who dismiss the whole thing with a shout. Some think the meaning of Zen is the state that has nothing to do with any of these assessments, and immediately leave when questioned.

None of these approaches lead to great enlightenment.

EFFECTS OF BUDDHISM

There are people who say they believe in Buddhism, or in Zen, who have practiced for years but without effect. The question is, what effects are they looking for?

Some people want to be known, or want to gain something for themselves. Some people pray to Buddhas and spirits to avert disaster and gain good fortune. Some people study in hopes of gaining knowledge. Some people perform esoteric practices to get supernatural powers. Some people practice arts and skills to outdo others. Some people practice curing in an effort to heal sickness. In such affairs, one may talk about effects or their absence, but the message of Zen is not on this order.

As far as the message of Zen is concerned, it has been said, "This is inherent in everyone, complete in every individual, not less in ordinary people, not more in sages." It is also said, "It is complete, like cosmic space, without lack or excess." If you think you get some effect from practicing Buddhism, this is like seeing excess in cosmic space; if you think there is no effect, this is like seeing lack in cosmic space. In either case you miss the point.

Among the most foolish of fools are people who worry that they will not get enlightened even if they practice Buddhism, who thus give up the idea before they even try because they do not want to waste the time and effort. What in the world is a guaranteed success? Those who want to get paid before they do any work, so to speak, who demand assurance of success before they make any effort, will never get anywhere, either in Buddhism or in ordinary endeavors.

ORIENTATION

An ancient Zen master said that Zen meditation is of no benefit if the application of mind is unclear. This does not mean that it is useless for unlearned people to do Zen meditation; it is a warning to those who sit in an ignorant fog and call that Zen meditation.

Some people say that Zen meditation is not accessible to the unlearned, so they should recite scriptures and incantations instead, because formal practices like recitations are easier and thus more conducive to realization. Scripture says, however, "If the orientation of mind is not correct, all practices are in vain."

This applies to Zen meditation as well as all formal practices. If the application of mind is correct, there will be no aberration in practices. Otherwise, all practices, whether formal or formless, concrete or abstract, are useless.

ZEN MEDITATION

Essential Zen meditation is not a matter of controlling thoughts and keeping the body immobile, so we cannot say that it is important to sit facing a wall and stop thinking. Also it is not a matter of contemplating doctrinal principles, so we cannot say it is important to learn doctrinal principles.

It does not require wealth, so we cannot say we are too poor to do it. It does not require physical strength, so we cannot say we are too weak to do it. It does not claim there is no Buddhism within worldly passions, so we cannot say that it is inaccessible to ordinary people.

Ceremonies and rituals are practices performed by the body, so it is impossible to do them when you are doing something else. Recitations and invocations are practices performed vocally, so these exercises must be set aside when you are talking about something else. Contemplation of principles is a practice performed by the intellect, so it does not get done when you are thinking about something else. But the Zen work is not done by the body, the speech, or the intellect; so what can be called important?

NOT EVEN MIND

Even if it is understood that Zen practice is not physical or verbal, there still arises a question about the statement that Zen is not mental performance either. If so, how is this to be reconciled with the presentation of instructions on mental application in Zen practice?

To say that Zen is not done physically, verbally, or intellectually does not mean that it consists of absence of thought, extinction of sense, or mortification of the body. The point is that the ordinary ideas of body and mind are illusions, and Zen avoids practicing rites, recitations, and contemplations based on ideas of body and mind as really existing. This is the point of the scriptural saying, "There is no eye, ear, nose, tongue, body, or mind."

One scripture says, "Enlightenment cannot be attained by the body, nor can it be attained by the mind. This is because both body and mind are like phantasms." Another scripture says, "Buddhahood cannot be attained by mind, Buddhahood cannot be attained by matter." The same scripture also says that Buddhahood cannot be attained by the body or by the intellect.

Ordinary people attribute perception to the senses, but Buddhism speaks of sensing independently of the ordinary sense organs. It is those who are unfamiliar with this principle who are disturbed by the statement that real Zen practice has nothing to do with acts of body, speech, or mind.

MINDLESS MENTAL APPLICATION

The various formal teachings and practices of Buddhism are designed as expedients to guide people according to their individual needs and potentials. They are formulated to lead people into the realm of enlightenment and are applied to the state where unenlightenment and enlightenment have already been distinguished.

Zen, in contrast, aims for the fundamental state, which is prior to this distinction. Therefore it does not admit of practices based on an existing dualism but points directly to the primordial unity underlying fabricated dualities. As the third patriarch of Zen said, "It is a mistake to apply the mind to the mind." The abstruse teaching of Zen is to "neither strive nor neglect."

NOT GETTING AWAY FROM THE SUBJECT

When people write poetry, they should understand the subject first. If you take up the subject of the moon, it will not do to think about flowers. The same is true in Buddhism.

Referring to the fundamental, Zen teaching says that it is not less in ordinary people or more in sages, that it is inherent in everyone and complete in every individual. If people take up the subject of the fundamental but then imagine that they are deluded and try to do some practice to become enlightened, then they are straying from the subject.

If people believe in the fundamental, they should not cling to the notion that they are deluded and seek enlightenment somewhere. Nevertheless, as long as they have not clearly experienced what is fundamentally complete in everyone, they should cast off their existing notions of distinction between delusion and enlightenment and look directly into the fundamental, either by themselves or in association with a teacher.

In the stories of enlightenment of ancient adepts, we do not read of anyone asking how to apply the mind in an effort to accord with the fundamental. They used to ask directly about what Buddha is, what Zen is, where Buddhas come from, and so on. Since the questions were direct, the answers they elicited were also direct, giving immediate indications of the fundamental.

These direct, immediate indications were not meant to be research materials or lessons for practice, but people who did not understand them used to dig into them, sometimes for many years. This process of sustained confrontation of pointers to the fundamental might be called practice or training, but it is not the same thing as defining understanding, practice, and realization and then cultivating various contemplations.

JUDGING THE WORDS OF ADEPTS

To make critical studies and judgments of the differences in the utterances of enlightened adepts is mundane vanity and idle sophistry. This arises from ignorance of the real nature and purpose of Zen sayings.

WONDER

Zen teachers may speak of wondering about Zen koans, or they may speak of not wondering about them. There is no fixed track for Zen teachers to follow.

Sometimes Zen teachers tell students to look at koans questioningly, sometimes they tell them not to doubt. In every case, a teacher is dealing directly with a student, not speaking in generalities.

Zen teachings are not doctrines kept in mind by the teachers. They are produced spontaneously at the interface between teacher and student. One should not try to freeze momentary teachings into fixed theories.

If Zen teachers are enlightened, their teaching may effectively take any form. If they are not enlightened, whatever form their teaching may take, it will actually blind their students.

KOANS

Sometimes Zen teachers give students koans to look at; sometimes they take koans away and have students abandon them. It is all a matter of method, not to be standardized.

When you become one with a koan, there is no one bringing up the koan and no koan being brought up. When you reach this stage, how can there be any dualism of giving and taking, using and not using?

Giving and taking away are methods temporarily used by teachers for students who have not yet reached this state. They cannot be judged by ordinary feelings.

When people without enlightenment formulate literalistic interpretations of Zen koans and hand on fixed doctrines to students, that is a big mistake. Such people were criticized by ancient masters for binding people with dogma.

NOT IN THE WORDS

Direct indications of the fundamental do not contain their intention in their literal expression. Therefore, students with keen faculties understand the import outside the words. In that case, how could there be any further discussion about the literal phrasing?

Duller students who linger over words find that they cannot figure them out intellectually. As long as their aspiration for enlightenment is unbending, their minds congeal in wonder. Some may break through this wonderment in a few days; others may take months, years, or even decades.

This congealed wonder puts a halt to compulsive intellectualizing, enabling the student to break through to a transconceptual mode of consciousness. This is why ancient Zen masters said that there is great enlightenment where there has been great wonder.

THE ORIGINS OF KOAN PRACTICE

The ancient Zen teachers did not tell students to take up their words as koans. They did not tell students to wonder at their words or not to wonder at them. Eventually, however, shallow people used to figure out the sayings of teachers intellectually and considered that enlightenment. Those who could not figure them out got bored and quit.

It was to help people like this that Chinese Zen masters from the eleventh century onward established the expedient device of calling a koan to mind without conceptualization. Even later on, for those unable to focus intense wonder on the koans, further methods were employed to foster the appropriate mood of inquiry.

ACTIVITY AND MEDITATION

People meditating on the fundamental carry out their ordinary tasks and activities in the midst of meditation and carry out meditation in the midst of ordinary tasks and activities. There is no disparity between meditation and activity.

It is for those as yet incapable of this, those weak in focusing their intent on the Way, that special meditation periods were set up. The practice of meditating four times a day in Zen communities began in this manner during the twelfth century.

In ancient times, Zen mendicants meditated twenty-four hours a day. In later times, however, there were those who became monks to avoid the trouble of making a living in the ordinary world. Their appetites distracted them from Buddhism, and when they participated in rituals their attention was taken away from the fundamental. Since these and other things inhibited them from work on the fundamental, they would have wasted their lives had not some other expedient been devised. This expedient was the rule of four daily periods of sitting meditation.

People who really have their minds on the Way, in contrast, do not forget work on the fundamental no matter what they are doing. Yet if they still distinguish this work from ordinary activities even as they do them together, they will naturally be concerned about being distracted by activities and forgetting the meditation work. This is because of viewing things as outside the mind.

An ancient master said, "The mountains, the rivers, the whole earth, the entire array of phenomena are all oneself." If you can absorb the essence of this message, there are no activities outside of meditation: you dress in meditation and eat in meditation; you walk, stand, sit, and lie down in meditation; you perceive and cognize in meditation; you experience joy, anger, sadness, and happiness in meditation.

Yet even this is still in the sphere of accomplishment and is not true merging with the source of Zen.

THE REASON FOR TEACHING RELINQUISHMENT

If it is granted that there is no distinction between meditation and ordinary activities, then it appears contradictory for Zen and other schools of Buddhism to urge students to let go of things and be aloof from objects.

An ancient master said, "The teaching has no fixed form; whatever you encounter is the source." The methods of teaching used by the wise to guide learners have no fixed form or appearance. Since it is a general principle of all universalistic Buddhist schools that there is no discrepancy between Buddhism and worldly phenomena, no genuine teachers could say there is practice of Buddhism outside of events and activities.

Nevertheless, because people who do not understand this entertain false ideas about things of the world, Zen teachers expediently tell them to relinquish things temporarily so as to enable them to get rid of their fixations.

ADJUSTMENT TO THE INDIVIDUAL

The father of the Buddha was a king. After his son attained Buddhahood and had begun to attract followers, the king had five hundred members of his clan become monks and nuns.

Hearing the Buddha tell his followers not to adorn their clothing or their dwelling places, one of these monks realized he could not follow the Teaching because as a member of a royal clan he was used to luxury.

The Buddha had a senior disciple go to the royal palace and obtain all sorts of finery to decorate a place for this monk, and had the monk stay there for the night. Because his usual cravings for luxury had been fulfilled, the monk's rambling thoughts spontaneously stopped and clarity of knowledge emerged. In the last part of the night, he attained sainthood.

The senior disciple was amazed by all of this and asked the Buddha about it. The Buddha said, "There are those whose attention to the Way is fostered by adorning their clothes and houses; for them, such adornment is an aid to enlightenment. Then again, there are those whose attention to the Way is diminished by fancy clothing and furnishings; these people should therefore beware of such things. Realization of the Way and attainment of its fruits depend entirely on the mentality of the practitioner, with no necessary relationship to such things as clothing and dwelling places."

So, for certain people, finery should not be prohibited as a hindrance to practice of the Way. But when people whose minds are not really on the Way of enlightenment use such examples to claim that indulgence in luxury is no hindrance to enlightenment, they are deluded.

LANDSCAPING

Since ancient times, there have been many people who have had special landscapes constructed for their enjoyment. Although the mood may be the same, there are differences of interest here.

Some people do not particularly care much for landscaping, themselves, but have it to adorn their houses, to impress other people and receive their compliments.

Some people are covetous in general and collect unusual rocks and trees as part of a hobby. Such people do not really appreciate the loveliness of landscape; they just like mundane objects.

A famous Chinese poet made a small pond and planted bamboo beside it, finding much delight in it. He wrote, "Because the heart of bamboo is open, it is my companion; because the nature of water is pure, it is my teacher." If people enjoy the landscape in the same spirit as that poet, they are not mere mundane sensualists.

There are also those who are by nature plain and aloof, who do not care much for mundane things but just nurture their minds writing poetry and reciting it in natural settings. These are the aesthetes. Yet even this, without the will for enlightenment, becomes a mundane routine.

Then again, some people turn to the mountains and rivers to rouse from slumber, clear their thoughts, and help them practice the Way. Their interest is not the same as that of ordinary people enjoying the landscape. They are to be respected, but as long as they have made a distinction between the landscape and the practice of the Way, they cannot be called genuine Wayfarers.

People who believe that the mountains, rivers, earth, plants, trees, and stones are all the fundamental Self may appear to appreciate the landscape through worldly feelings, but there are those who eventually make those worldly feelings into the will for enlightenment and make the changing appearances of the springs, rocks, plants, and trees through the four seasons into meditation work. That is how Wayfarers appreciate the landscape.

So it is not necessarily bad to like landscape and not necessarily good. There is no plus or minus in the landscape itself; gain and loss are in people's attitudes.

ZEN, TEA, AND THE ARTS

In China, tea is drunk for health. Just as an overdose of medicine causes trouble, tea should not be taken to excess.

In ancient times, tea was valued as a stimulant to banish drowsiness and help people study. The founder of Zen in Japan also liked tea for its stimulating effect, to help people practice the Way.

Later on, however, the use of tea for health purposes, or for study, gave way to frivolous overuse. This also created extra expense and led to neglect of Buddhism.

The liking for tea may itself be one and the same, therefore, but whether it is beneficial or harmful depends on the attitude of the individual.

This principle also applies to the arts. The original

purpose of the arts is to tune and refine the mind. Once they become objects of personal attachment, however, their refining action is lost and they turn into occasions for perversion and corruption.

It is for this reason that Buddhist teachers sometimes say that there is no way to meditate outside of life's activities, and sometimes they encourage people to set activities aside in order to meditate.

SUPRANORMAL POWERS OF THE ENLIGHTENED

People wonder whether the enlightened necessarily have supranormal powers. The fact is that even sorcerers and magicians with no concept of liberation also can learn to operate supranormal powers, so the presence of such powers does not in itself indicate enlightenment. Even Buddhist saints with supranormal powers are not considered fully enlightened before they have realized the totality of the teaching.

There is an ancient Buddhist saying, "Even if you have all the supranormal powers, you should know there is still one more power." That "one more power" is in all beings; all capacities, perceptions, and activities are beholden to this power. Unaware of this, ordinary people seek externally for mundane powers. The absorption in the universal treasury of light spoken of in scripture is the spiritual light inherent in all living beings. All the auras, knowledge, and powers of Buddhas come from this treasury of light; all perception and discernment are functions of this light.

LETTING GO

To think that Zen practice means abandoning all understanding is a big mistake. As an ancient said, "It cannot be sought consciously, yet cannot be found in unconsciousness; it cannot be reached by words, yet cannot be comprehended by silence."

Even among Zen students there are those who make literal interpretation of ancient sayings about nonattachment and think that the message of Zen is to ignore all meaning and principle, not define distinctions in stages, and not keep either Buddhism or worldly realities in mind. The ancients ridiculed this, calling it "spade Zen," because a spade is used to dig things out, representing the misconception that the teaching of Zen is to abandon all understanding.

THE FUNDAMENTAL GROUND

The fundamental ground is a term provisionally applied to the point where illusion and enlightenment are as yet undifferentiated, to which no worldly names or descriptions apply, and which even transmundane teachings do not reach.

This state is also called the one great matter, the original face, and the master within. These are just provisional names, set up to induce confused people to see the reality.

BUDDHA NATURE

Buddhism talks about the ground of mind, or the Buddha nature, in the context of division between ordinary people and Buddhas. This is not the same as the Zen definition of the fundamental ground, which is prior to the division between ordinary people and Buddhas.

Once you realize the fundamental ground, however, then the Buddha nature, the ground of mind, the matrix of realization of thusness, true suchness, the nature of reality and even the objects seen by ordinary people, all become the fundamental ground.

WHERE IS IT?

An ancient said, "It is always there, right where you are; if you seek it, obviously you do not see it." The fundamental ground is not inside the body and mind, nor is it outside the body and mind. Nor can it be said that the total body-mind is the fundamental ground.

It is not in the categories of sentience or insentience, it

is not the knowledge of Buddhas and saints. The knowledge of Buddhas and saints, as well as the bodies and minds of sentient beings and even their worlds and lands, all come from this; that is why it is provisionally called the fundamental ground.

The Diamond Sutra says, "The Buddhas and the Buddhas' teaching of supreme perfect enlightenment all come from this 'scripture.'" This adamantine insight is the fundamental ground.

The Complete Enlightenment Sutra says, "All pure suchness, enlightenment, nirvana, and the transcendent ways flow forth from complete awareness." This complete awareness is the fundamental ground.

REACHING THE
FUNDAMENTAL GROUND

Since the fundamental ground is neither a feature of the world nor a transmundane phenomenon, many people who want to practice Zen wonder how it can be reached. This question itself, however, indicates a failure to digest the implications of the term *fundamental.*

If you associate the fundamental with a worldly art, then you will wonder what skill or technique you should learn in order to attain it. If you suppose the fundamental to be a transmundane phenomenon, then you will wonder how you can realize it without knowledge.

Once you have heard of what is neither a mundane nor a transmundane thing, you are foolish to wonder how to reach it. To reach the fundamental ground is not something like going from the country to the city or from one land to another. In reality it is like waking up from a dream. All the questions about where the fundamental ground is and how to get there are part of the dream, arising from the thoughts of a dream about a dream.

Even if you have not awakened, if you realize that your perceptions and activities are all like dreams and you view them with detachment, not giving rise to grasping and rejecting discrimination, then this is virtually tantamount to awakening from the dream; at least you may be said to believe in the existence of reality.

In the fundamental ground, there is no sign of ordinariness or sainthood, no purity or defilement. Because of the "dream" of consciousness conditioned by unconscious habit, purity and defilement appear in the midst of formlessness, and one sees distinctions between the ordinary and the holy in the midst of the uncreated. When you think you are an ordinary mortal, you go running around after honor and gain, disappointed if you do not get them. When you think you are wise, you look down on everyone and develop a conceited attitude. When you are fooled by such delusions, you do not even believe in the existence of a fundamental ground of peace and happiness, let alone experience it.

The Complete Enlightenment Sutra says, "People mistake the material elements for their own bodies and take reflections of the objects of the six senses for their own minds. This is like diseased eyes seeing flowers in the sky, or a second moon. This is why they arbitrarily pursue the repetitious routines by which they live and die. That is called ignorance. Ignorance has no real substance; it is like seeing someone in a dream. It is not that there is no presence, but on awakening, that person is not there."

The Heroic Progress Sutra says, "The subtle essence is complete clarity beyond all name or description. Originally there are no worlds, no sentient beings." All the Universalist Buddhist scriptures speak in this vein; why disbelieve in this and instead wear out your body and mind in external seeking?

MIND AND SELF

In the Indian philosophy known as Sankhya, everything in the world is classified into twenty-five realities. The first is called the Unknown Reality. Prior to the division of heaven and earth, not in the realm of good or bad, beyond the range of perception and cognition—it is only called the Unknown Reality for lack of a better term. It is eternal, unaffected by change and decay.

The twenty-fifth reality is called the Reality of the

Spiritual Self. The twenty-three realities between the first and the twenty-fifth are the forms of various good and bad changes, which are called compounded phenomena. If the spiritual self produces feelings of good and bad, the Unknown Reality changes to manifest corresponding appearances. If the spiritual self produces ideas such as long and short, round and square, the Unknown Reality changes to manifest such forms.

Thus, all compounded and changeable worldly things depend on the production of feelings by the spiritual self. If the spiritual self produces no feelings and reverts to the Unknown Reality, the changing of compounds stops forever, and effortless peace and happiness ensue. Even though the material body dies, the spiritual self is eternal and unperishing.

The foregoing is a worldview repudiated by realized Buddhists. There are Taoists, however, who share a similar philosophy. Lao-tzu's "Nothingness" and Chuang-tzu's "Uncontrived Great Tao" correspond to the Unknown Reality.

Some followers of Buddhism also cling to such a view. According to *The Complete Enlightenment Sutra,* "When a jewel reflects five colors, fools think the jewel itself is actually five-colored. In the same way, when the forms of body and mind temporarily appear in the pure nature of complete awareness, the ignorant are deluded into thinking they really have these physical and mental characteristics. That is why body and mind are called illusory defilement."

A great teacher of old said, "The loss of spiritual wealth and ruination of virtue invariably come from mind, intellect, and consciousness." A classical Zen master said, "The reason students of the Way do not know the Real is that they have only recognized the conscious spirit too long."

When beginners first practice the so-called Zen meditation of inward gazing, on perceiving the formless, boundless, radiant awareness of the mind, they think this is the "master within" or the "original face." Ancient Zen teachers ridiculed this belief as "playing with the spirit" and "recognizing the conscious spirit." *The Complete Enlightenment Sutra* also refers to this as "taking a thief to be your own child."

Buddha said that all worlds are just one mind, that there is nothing outside of mind. There are different interpretations about what the term *one mind* means.

People in the small vehicles of Buddhism suppose that the thinking of the conceptual consciousness is the "one mind." In the Great Vehicle, two more subtle consciousnesses are brought to light. Since the teaching says all phenomena are transfigurations of eight kinds of consciousness, people think the statement that all worlds are mind refers to the eighth consciousness, which is called the repository consciousness, or the so-called monarch of mind. Some also define a ninth consciousness and say that all phenomena are manifestations of consciousness conforming to conditions, and that this is the reason all worlds are said to be one mind.

Students of the small vehicles do not know of the subtle consciousness in mind, so as long as thoughts of attachment and discrimination do not arise in relation to objects, they think this is the ultimate.

As for students of the Great Vehicle, there are those who think that the original mind is where you do not get involved in discrimination of objects but just see mountains as mountains and rivers as rivers, without clinging to right or wrong or good or bad. This, however, is the element of the primary five sense consciousnesses within the conceptual consciousness; it is not the original mind.

The reality of mind is inconceivable. To extend throughout the universe does not stretch it, and to enter into a minute object does not cramp it. It is beyond all forms, yet contains all forms. It is imbued with boundless virtues, yet is not within its boundless virtues. Therefore, you cannot even divide true and false; you can hardly talk about crude and subtle.

Nevertheless, as long as you are confused or deluded, the true and the false are not equal, the crude and the subtle are not on a par. In spite of this fact, when people who have still not gotten away from confused and deluded views hear sayings like "Mind itself is Buddha," they interpret it literally to mean that arbitrary feelings and emotions are themselves the Buddha-mind. Although the saying seems Buddhist, the interpretation is false. This has been explained in many Buddhist texts for just such people.

Even if you are not enlightened, as long as you understand the principle clearly, you are not likely to make the mistake of "taking a fish eye for a pearl."

Because of their shallow background, people of later ages who studied Buddhist doctrines thought that the ultimate point was to learn the passages expounding the principle of mind in the literature of the various schools; they did not themselves realize the source of mind.

People who go into Zen think this is all doctrinal talk and suppose that Zen practitioners shouldn't study it. If you genuinely let go of *both* worldly illusions *and* transcendental teachings, and truly head for unexcelled enlightenment—*this* is what Zen encourages. It is a mistake, however, to avoid studying scriptures and just follow your own imaginations and ideas to recognize the conscious spirit, mistaking it for the original mind.

TRUE AND FALSE MIND

It is hard to give a simple definition of the distinction between true and false. It is a mistake to say the true mind and the false mind are the same, and yet it is also mistaken to say they are different.

Suppose you press your eyeball with your finger, causing yourself to see a doubled image, such as a second moon beside the real moon. Now this second moon is only seen because of the pressure of the finger on your eye; there isn't really any second moon beside the real moon.

This does not mean, however, that if you don't want to be seeing a second moon, you should get rid of the false moon and see the real moon. If you simply remove the finger pressing your eyeball, there is no other moon beside the original moon. If you try to get rid of the second moon without removing the finger from your eye, you will never succeed.

There are some people who think there is no real moon apart from this second moon, so they are in love with it. That is also a big mistake.

Those who do not put pressure on their eyeballs do not see a second moon to begin with; how could there be any debate about whether or not to get rid of the second moon? So the issue of the sameness or difference of the true and false mind arises because of pressing the eye of the fundamental with the finger of confusion.

TWO BASES

In *The Heroic Progress Sutra* the Buddha says, "The reason people have unnecessarily been subject to repetitive routines since beginningless time is that they have lost their original mind and think that the conceptually cognizing mind is their own mind. Therefore, even if they happen to practice the teaching of Buddha, since they are ignorant of the two bases and thus practice mistakenly, they fall into aberrant states.

"The first of the two bases is the original pure essence of the subtle luminosity of fundamental awareness. This is the source of the minds of all beings. They have forgotten this basis.

"The second is the basis of beginningless repetitive routine. This is your idea that cogitation and conceptualization are your own mind. If you cultivate spiritual practice with this mind, it may become another routine activity, but it will not get you to the source, just as boiling sand will not make rice, no matter how long you cook it; you will only get hot sand, not rice."

In Master Huisi's *Treatise on Stopping and Seeing According to the Great Vehicle* it says, "There are two kinds of characteristics of mind. One is real, the second is false. The substance of the real mind is suchness as is; thoroughly pure and perfectly complete, it pervades everywhere and produces all things. The false mind is discriminatory cognition that has no real substance but produces falsehoods."

THE CONDITIONED MIND AND
THE NATURAL MIND

All material and mental phenomena have a distinction between the conditioned and the natural. Temporal manifestations arising from the combination of factors are called conditioned. Essential qualities inherent in the matrix of realization of suchness are called natural.

Conditioned fire has no actual substance, but it performs its function under appropriate conditions. When fire is used properly, it has great benefits, such as preventing chill and cooking food. When fire is used carelessly, it does great harm, such as burning houses and destroying goods. To teach people how to use fire properly is thus beneficial to the world.

Even if you use fire according to instructions, however, you still do not know natural, ever-present essential fire. If you want to know this essential fire, you need to avoid fixing your attention on the harm and help of conditioned fire.

The same is true of the reality of mind. Even though the conditioned illusory mind has no real substance, if it does wrong it falls into bad tendencies and suffers all sorts of misery, and if it does good it is reconstituted in good states and experiences all sorts of happiness. Even among ordinary people and cultists there are those who, realizing this principle, restrain the mind from doing anything bad. Even though they may be temporarily born in pleasant states by training the conditioned mind, as long as they do not know the original mind, they cannot avoid compulsive routines.

Even saints and sages who have only reformed the errors of the illusory mind and turned them into illusory knowledge, without attaining accord with the original mind, are not free of change. This is like using conditional fire properly; therefore the sutras of *Complete Enlightenment* and *Heroic Progress* explain the existence of essential fire apart from conditioned fire, the existence of mind apart from the conditioned mind.

In the teachings of non-Zen schools of Buddhism, there is talk about temporarily producing illusory knowledge to put an end to illusory confusion, then spontaneously attaining accord with the fundamental after that. Even the *Complete Enlightenment* and *Heroic Progress* sutras also say that after producing illusory knowledge to get rid of illusory confusion, one should reach a nonillusory state where object and knowledge are both forgotten.

Some people who study Buddhism think that this talk about illusory knowledge is the fundamental intention of the Buddhas and Zen masters. *The Complete Enlightenment Sutra* says, "As the illusory body vanishes, the illusory mind also vanishes; as the illusory mind vanishes, illusory objects also vanish. As illusory objects vanish, illusory vanishing also vanishes. As illusory vanishing vanishes, the nonillusory does not vanish. It is like polishing a mirror;

when the grime is gone, the clarity appears. Body and mind are both illusory grime; when the grime is gone, everywhere is clear and pure."

Some people who misinterpret this passage and who still have not realized the original mind think that extinguishing body and mind and being empty and quiet is real Buddhism. This is the extinction trance of the lesser vehicles of individual salvation and the imageless trance of the Hindus. It is like hearing that conditional fire is not true fire, then imagining real fire to be the darkness resulting from extinction of all conditional fire.

MIND AND ESSENCE

It is said that the founder of Zen came from India to China, where he did not set up writings but pointed directly to the mind so people would see its essence and realize enlightenment. The teachings of Mahayana Buddhism all say one's own mind is Buddha. Why is it said that you attain Buddhahood by seeing essence, rather than that you attain Buddhahood by seeing mind?

Once someone asked a great Zen master of China about the distinction between mind and essence. The master said, "When it's cold, water freezes into ice; when it's warm, ice melts into water. Similarly, when you are confused, essence freezes into mind; when you are enlightened, mind melts into essence. Mind and essence are the

same, but they differ according to confusion and enlightenment."

Even though it is made by a great Zen master, this
explanation of the distinction between mind and essence
is also a temporary one, which should not be taken too
literally.

There are many meanings to the word *essence*. Three
meanings are provisionally explained in Buddhism.

One is the meaning of unvarying. The essences of pepper and sweet grass, for example, are different; pepper is
not sweet, sweet grass is not pungent.

Second is the meaning of distinction. This refers to the
distinct natures of animate and inanimate beings.

Third is the meaning of real essence. This refers to
the fundamental source of all phenomena, the nondual
inherent essence.

Zen is a special transmission outside of doctrine. Even
though we talk of seeing essence, it does not mean the
real essence as spoken of in the doctrinally based schools.
That which is fundamental in every human being cannot
be called mind and cannot be called essence. Nevertheless,
using these words *mind* and *essence* in order to get people
to know the fundamental, we sometimes speak of one
mind and sometimes talk about one essence.

In the expression "Directly pointing to the human
mind, to see its essence and realize enlightenment," we use
the word *essence* instead of *mind* in order to let it be known

that what ordinary confused people think is mind is like a second moon.

Even though we say "See essence," that does not mean it is to be seen with the eyes. Neither is it to be understood by mind and consciousness. Attaining enlightenment does not mean beatification and radiating an aura of light; it is like a drunken man coming to his senses. When confusion and delusion suddenly stop and you meet the fundamental directly, this is called seeing essence and realizing enlightenment.

A great Zen master said, "Zen teachers with no eyes all make the mistake of pointing to the human mind, saying it is essence and claiming that this is getting people to realize enlightenment." There are teachers who just explain the meanings and principles of mind and essence and think that teaching this to others is "direct pointing." Some students think that understanding these doctrines is attainment of truth. This ought to be called explaining essence, not seeing essence.

UNREALITY AND REALITY IN THINGS

Some Buddhist scriptures say all things are unreal, while others say all things are eternal features of reality. In the fundamental, however, there is no sign of permanence and no sense of unreality. Nevertheless, things are said to be unreal the way ordinary people see them, yet eternal as saints see them.

Someone who is really enlightened, however, has neither the view of the ordinary mortal nor the view of the saint. That means all talk about unreality or eternity is expedient method.

In *The Lankavatara Sutra*, a Hindu asks Buddha, "Are phenomena all impermanent?"

The Buddha replies, "Your question is mundane sophistry."

The Hindu then asks, "Are all things then eternal?"

The Buddha replies, "This question is also mundane sophistry."

In *The Sutra Spoken by Vimalakirti*, it says, "Do not use the fluctuating mind to discuss the characteristics of reality." If people talk about the meaning of the real character of things without changing their conventional views, it is all sophistry.

This is what is meant by the saying, "If the wrong person preaches a right teaching, even a right teaching becomes wrong. If the right person expounds a wrong teaching, even a wrong teaching becomes right."

ORDINARY AND SPIRITUAL VIEWS

There are various descriptions of ordinary and spiritual views in the Buddhist teachings. In *The Heroic Progress Sutra,* for example, there is an explanation of seven universal elements. These elements are earth, water, fire, air, space, senses, and consciousness. These seven universal elements, as inherent qualities of the matrix of realization of thusness, pervade the cosmos freely. These are called essential fire, essential air, and so forth.

Shingon Buddhism teaches that six all-pervasive universal elements form the substance of all phenomena. This is the same idea as that of the Sutras, though the Shingon doctrine does not talk about the universal element of senses. The universal element of senses refers to the six senses pervading the cosmos.

In Shingon Buddhism, the six universal elements are considered the body of the cosmos. In *The Heroic Progress Sutra,* the matrix of realization of thusness is considered the body of the cosmos, with the explanation that the seven universal elements are qualities and functions inherent in the matrix of realization of thusness. Both are expedient teachings of Buddha.

Even though Shingon speaks of six universal elements, this does not refer to conditioned water, fire, and so on; it is the essential fire, essential water, and so on, as spoken of in *The Heroic Progress Sutra.* The four mandalas of Shingon

Buddhism refer to all conditioned phenomena. Thus the six universal elements are called the substance, the four mandalas are called the form, and the three mysteries are called the function.

In each of the seven universal elements, there is the distinction between the inherent quality and the conditioned arising. If you understand one element thoroughly first, the others will be understood as well.

Fire produced in the world, by means such as drilling wood or striking sparks from stone, is conditioned fire. This fire is insubstantial; it cannot burn without fuel of some kind. When the proper conditions are present, such as fuel, the fire temporarily appears; therefore it is said to be insubstantial. In all the Buddhist scriptures, exoteric and esoteric, it is unanimously stated that conditionally produced phenomena have no real substantiality.

As for essential fire, it pervades the cosmos, neither burning nor going out.

Ordinary people see only conditional fire and do not know essential fire. If you know essential fire, you do not have to reject conditional fire, because conditional fire is a function of essential fire.

The other universal elements are like the element of fire, including the universal element of consciousness, which is the mental consciousness of sentient beings. In this case too, what ordinary people usually think is mind is actually the conditioned mind. This conditioned mind has no real substance; it just has temporary appearances of perception and cognition due to the conditions of the fields of data associated with the six senses. This is like conditional fire temporarily burning because of the presence of fuel.

Ignorant people know only the conditioned mind and do not know the essential mind. The mind spoken of in non-Buddhist books and lesser vehicle Buddhist teachings is the conditioned mind. Even the Great Vehicle doctrine of the eighth consciousness is still in the domain of the conditioned mind. That is why a ninth consciousness is defined in the ultimate great vehicle, to indicate the universal element of consciousness as an inherent quality.

All phenomena are either mental or material. Among the seven universal elements, the element of consciousness is mental, the other six are material. Nevertheless, since the seven elements interpenetrate freely in the matrix of realization of thusness, there is no distinction between matter and mind. This is called the true cosmos, the realm of reality.

Even though they have no distinction, matter and mind are not mixed up. Therefore material reality is not the forms and appearances that appear and disappear, flourish and wane; mental reality has no changes of motion and stillness, activation and extinction. This is the sense in which scriptures say that the real characteristics of all things are permanent.

When ordinary people develop false views, the matrix of realization of thusness manifests the appearances of material and mental phenomena in accordance with the falsehoods. Because the false views of ordinary people fluctuate, so also do perceptions and phenomena have changing appearances. It is like when you travel down the river in a boat and it looks like the riverbank is moving. It is also like a profusion of flowers appearing in the sky to clouded eyes. This is the sense in which scriptures say that all phenomena are unreal.

So it is sometimes said that all things are unreal, sometimes that all things are eternal. The statements may be different, but the phenomena themselves are the same. Those who do not know the Buddha's intention grasp one and reject the other, according to the difference in statement. That is all mundane sophistry.

When someone with clouded eyes and someone with clear eyes are in the same place facing open space, a welter of flowers appear to the one with clouded eyes, while the one with clear eyes sees the very same place as open space. This is the sense in which it is said that affliction is enlightenment, samsara is nirvana, and the state of eternity, the ineffable, is none other than the original state.

Sayings referring to present appearances as the Tao and to things themselves as reality also refer to this perspective. It is a big mistake to understand this to mean that you attain the knowledge and vision of Buddhas while still keeping the views of ordinary people. Why else would special religious disciplines be established?

DISTINCTIONS IN BUDDHIST TEACHING

In absolute reality there are no distinctions between greater and lesser vehicles or between temporary and true teachings. Because of the differences in the intelligence of students, however, there are distinctions in the teachings they understand.

The Lotus Sutra says, "Although the teaching of the Buddha is one, because the natures and inclinations of sentient beings differ, the avenues to truth they understand are also different. It is like one and the same rain falling from the sky being absorbed differently by the plants and trees according to the size of their roots and stems, branches and leaves."

THE SCHOOLS OF ZEN

The reason for the division of Zen into five schools was not that there are so many levels of attainment; it was because of differences in methods used to guide learners to the fundamental.

Sometimes Zen teachers talk about ultimate principle, sometimes they demonstrate keys of potential. These are not intellectual or sentimental interpretations; they are called the barriers of the Zen founders.

A great Zen teacher of China said, "Even if people have true awakening and true realization, as long as they have not understood the whole truth, they blind people when they expound their personal realization to them."

Once a government official called on a Zen master and asked about the Zen manners of teaching. The master said, "The manners of our school are not subjectively comprehensible. Nevertheless, the general idea may be discerned in a certain poem about a beautiful lady, written by a woman:

'Trying unsuccessfully to depict the scene,
In her chamber she sets forth her sadness.
Though she calls her maid over and over, there is
    no matter;
She just wants her man to recognize her voice.' "

The woman's man is her secret lover, who comes to her stealthily. When he comes near where she lives, the woman wants to let him know she is in her boudoir, but she is worried about gossip, so she keeps calling her maid, not because there is something to do but just to let her man know by the sound of her voice that she is in her room. The manners of the five schools of Zen are also like this; literary criticisms of the words used to "call the maid" miss the original intent of the Zen teachers.

PRAISE AND CENSURE IN ZEN

When authentic Zen masters praise and censure each other, these too are methods of "calling the maid." This is not the same thing as making evaluations based on human sentiments and egocentric attachments.

EXPEDIENT TEACHINGS

From the Zen point of view, all of Buddha's teachings are methods of "calling the maid." Sometimes he said all things are impermanent, sometimes he said all things are everlasting. Sometimes he said all things are unreal, sometimes he said all things are characteristics of reality. Sometimes he said all writings are not enlightened teaching, sometimes he said all verbalization is the body of reality. The fundamental intent of the Buddha is not in any such statements, but people ignorant of the Buddha's intention pick out words that suit their subjective feelings and believe these are the Buddha's fundamental intention.

A sutra says, "When the spirit of fire enters into water, water also becomes fire. When the spirit of water enters into fire, fire also becomes water." This is the way it is with Buddhism: when seen with the eye of Zen, the doctrinal teachings also turn into the message of Zen; when seen with the eye of the doctrines, the message of Zen and the doctrinal teachings are no different.

This is true not only of the distinction between doctrine and Zen; it is also true of Buddhism and things of the world. When the insightful understanding of Buddhism is opened up, the features of the world are all Buddhist teachings. As long as you have not escaped mundane sentiments, even what you have understood as the profoundest of subtle principles is also a worldly thing.

ZEN AND DOCTRINE

Doctrinal schools of Buddhism define the teachings of Buddhism variously as being adapted to others or as being according to the Buddha's own intent. When Zen teachers use this distinction, it is just a method of "calling the maid," not a fixed dogma. What they may say today is spoken according to Buddha's own intent; what they may say tomorrow is adapted to others.

This also applies to teachings such as "shallow strategy" and "profound secret," "verbal expression of arbitrary attachments" and "verbal expression in conformity to meaning." An ancient said, "The message of Zen is not like the teachings of the doctrinal schools, in which one foot is one foot and two feet are two feet."

Buddha did not call himself either a teacher of doctrine or a teacher of Zen; his teachings cannot really be divided into part doctrine and part Zen either. That is because the inner experience of Buddhas is neither doctrine nor

Zen. Distinctions between doctrine and Zen are created by the function of this inner experience as it responds to circumstances.

It says in a sutra, "Buddha speaks the truth with one voice, while sentient beings interpret it differently, according to type." Although there were differences in understanding during the lifetime of Buddha, there was no division into followers of Zen or meditation and followers of doctrine. After the Buddha passed away, there was a division into Zen and doctrines; the doctrines included various schools, exoteric and esoteric, while Zen was differentiated into five houses.

The reason for this was that people with great knowledge and lofty virtue, successors to the teaching of Buddha, first set forth expedients according to the natures and inclinations of people with various understandings, in order to convey the basic message of Buddha to them. Some became teachers of doctrine, some became teachers of Zen, each putting forth a hand to break through the biased attachments of the deluded, transcend the duality of doctrines and Zen, and lead to the fundamental ground.

Therefore, the basic intent of genuine doctrinal teachers is not in the doctrines, and the basic intent of clear-eyed Zen teachers is not in Zen. The differences in what they say are due to the variety of methods they use for "calling the maid." In later ages, students of Zen and the doctrines who put biased attachments first sank into the sea of affirmation and denial, obscuring the original meaning of the Buddha and the Zen founders.

In *The Sutra on Settling Doubts about Imitation Teaching* it says, "Literalism is the enemy of the Buddhas of past, present, and future." Genuine teachers with clear eyes do not have prepackaged dogmas stored up in their chests; they just speak out according to the potential of the situation, without any fixed slogans.

When people ask about Zen, masters may reply with sayings of Confucius or Mencius, or Lao-tzu or Chuang-tzu; or sometimes they may reply with teachings of the doctrinal schools of Buddhism. Sometimes they use proverbs to answer, sometimes they use objects at hand. The methods of masters are called the living play of Zen; they cannot be judged by the feelings and perceptions of those who have not reached this state.

PURE LAND BUDDHISM

Among masters of the various schools of Buddhism, including Zen Buddhism, have been those who encouraged the Pure Land Buddhist practice of chanting the name of the Buddha of Infinite Light. Some types of Pure Land Buddhist teaching and practice are elementary and incomplete, but this is a matter of perspective. *The Nirvana Sutra* says, "Coarse words and fine speech all end up in ultimate truth." *The Lotus Sutra* says, "Productive labor and business do not contravene the character of reality." When you have awakened to the principle of the Great Vehicle, then all talk in the world, all activity, is the Great Vehicle of Perfect Meaning; so recitation of a Buddha name could hardly be called a lesser vehicle.

The masters who set up Pure Land Buddhism understood the profound principle of the Great Vehicle in their own minds, yet temporarily distinguished the Pure Land from the defiled land in order to guide ignorant people, drawing a distinction between self-power and Other-power. They were not ignorant themselves; these teachings are compassionate expedients of enlightening beings.

Among believers in Pure Land Buddhism, however, there are those who invoke the Buddha's name with the notion that there is a Pure Land outside this defiled land. This cannot be called the Great Vehicle of Perfect Meaning.

While there are incomplete teachings in the Buddha's own discourses, they are expedients for guidance, so they should not be considered useless. The reason that certain sutras seem to scorn the incomplete teachings is to let people know that the fundamental intent of the Buddha is in the complete teachings.

There is also a secret teaching of Buddha invocation in the Shingon (Mantra) school of Buddhism, which is not the same as the interpretation of Pure Land Buddhists.

Zen practitioners also recite Buddha names, but the focus of their attention is different from that of ordinary practitioners of Buddha invocation.

There is no fixed form of practice in Zen. The custom of reciting certain spells is a recent development. There is also no fixed icon; people recite sacred names according to the image used to focus their attention.

Some believers in Zen think that Pure Land Buddhism is an inferior vehicle and consider practitioners of Buddha-remembrance to be ignorant people. Thus they reject the Pure Land practice altogether; but this is really because they do not understand the Zen teaching that its message is in everyone. *The Sutra on Consideration of Benefit* says, "Hearing the teaching of the Great Vehicle, there are those who disbelieve and reject it. This is like an ignoramus taking a disliking to space itself and trying to get out of it. A bystander who takes pity on the ignoramus and tries to call him back into space is also an ignoramus. So is the one who pities those who have abandoned the Great Vehicle and tries to get them into it."

SPECIALIZATION

People who really believe in Zen know that all doings and activities are none other than Zen, so they sometimes practice Buddha-remembrance and read sutras and spells. Pure Land practice done in this spirit is fine for Zen practitioners too, but those Pure Land followers who think chanting a Buddha's name is the only right practice contravene the true principle of the Great Vehicle. Similarly, Zennists who think zazen is the only right practice are also mistaken. Nevertheless, it may be useful for beginners to concentrate on one practice to the exclusion of others, but only as a temporary measure.

ZEN PRAISE, ZEN BLAME

Zen teachers with clear eyes may sometimes praise ancient masters and may sometimes blame them. This is not actually aimed at the ancient masters but is, rather, a technique employed for the benefit of the learner.

An ancient said, "You are no different from the Buddhas and Zen masters." To people with clear eyes, there is no Buddhahood or mastery to worship, and no ordinariness to despise. Nevertheless, they use all sorts of methods to help people actually reach this fundamental ground where there is no division between the ordinary person and the sage. Sometimes they praise, sometimes they blame, but their intention is not in praise and blame at all.

Ignorant students who do not know this follow the words literally and get happy when praised and angry or guilty when blamed. Those claiming to be teachers who may speak of the nondivision between the ordinary person and the sage but have not really reached this state will praise and blame based on dogmatic views of appearances of right and wrong in students. *The Sutra of Complete Enlightenment* says, "People who study enlightenment in the degenerate age may gain a little bit of realization without having gotten rid of the root of the self-image; therefore they like people who believe their doctrine and resent people who criticize it."

SHARPNESS AND DULLNESS

Although it may be said, from the Zen point of view, that there is no difference between the ordinary mortal and the sage, nevertheless distinctions are still drawn between those of sharp faculties and those of dull faculties, between perceptive and unperceptive teachers. These distinctions are not made according to conventional arguments but are based on the Zen viewpoint.

Those who do not believe they are no different from Buddhas even when they have understood all the teachings are said to have dull faculties. This does not mean, however, that there really exists such a thing as an ignorant person totally alien to enlightenment. Those who think of themselves as more enlightened than others and set themselves up as teachers based on self-attachment and religious attachment are called unperceptive teachers. This does not mean, however, that there are people who are fundamentally stupid and intrinsically inferior to perceptive teachers.

These teachings are not susceptible to understanding by sentimental or intellectual senses; they are only known to those who reach this state.

ZEN MEDITATION

Meditation is practiced in both Buddhist and non-Buddhist schools. Experience of the realms of pure form and formlessness comes from the power of meditation concentration; cultists cultivate these as the ultimate end.

The word *zen* originally meant "meditation," but this does not refer to cultivation of the meditation practices of other schools. Because the practice, if not the theory, of meditation became rare in other schools, people came to think of it as a specialty of Zen.

The Lankavatara Sutra expounds four kinds of meditation. First is the meditation practiced by the ignorant, ordinary cultists who think that meditation concentration means not producing thoughts and not giving rise to discrimination. Second is meditation examining characteristics and meanings, where Buddhists in elementary and middling grades of attainment examine and contemplate the principles of the teachings. Third is Zen focused on reality as is, where advanced Buddhists dwell in the reality of the Middle Way in its true aspect, subtle practice not requiring effort. Fourth is the pure meditation that comes from suchness, where one enters into the state of the realization of thusness, and self-realized higher knowledge emerges.

JUDGING TEACHERS AND TEACHINGS

There are many false teachings current confusing authentic Buddhism. In sports and games, there are formally established criteria of winning and losing, so there is no confusion in judging them. In civil and criminal legal disputes, it may be hard to determine right and wrong, but they can be settled by appeal to higher authorities.

Buddhism, in contrast, has no such predetermined winning or losing. People all think, based on what they themselves have individually understood, that the doctrine they follow is best, even though others do not agree. There is no authority to which to appeal; though the proofs people adduce may be the words of Buddha and Zen masters, since the interpretation of literature changes according to the views people hold to, it is not sufficient as a basis of proof. People also take the approval of the teachers they believe in as proof, but the testimony of an interested party is not trustworthy.

In any case, unenlightened people think that the beliefs they imagine to be true are fundamental, so once they come to believe in any doctrine of any school, they reject all other schools. Once they have come to believe in someone as their own guru, some people think everyone else's doctrine is inferior and even refuse to hear anything else. Such people are the stupidest of imbeciles.

There are also those who remain hesitant and indecisive because the teachings of various schools and teachers differ.

Foods have many flavors; which one could be defined as quintessential? As people's constitutions differ, so do their tastes. Some people like sweets, some like peppery foods. If you said the flavor *you* like is *the* quintessential flavor and the rest are useless, you would be an imbecile. So it is with Buddhist teachings: because people's natural inclinations differ, it may be that a particular teaching is especially valuable to a given individual, but it becomes false if one clings to it as the unique and only truth, to the exclusion of all other teachings.

The Lotus Sutra says, "The spiritual monarch breaking through existence emerged in the world teaching in various ways according to people's natures and inclinations." We should realize that the various doctrines and methods taught by the Buddha were provisionally expounded in accord with people's confused and deluded natures and inclinations.

As for those who turn directly to the fundamental that is prior to the division between ordinary people and Buddhas, even if they hear all sorts of doctrines, why would they trouble their minds over judgments of superiority and inferiority? An ancient said, "The reason the Buddhas expounded all the teachings was to liberate all minds. Since I have no mind at all, what do I need with any of the teachings?"

Printed in the United States
by Baker & Taylor Publisher Services